This book belongs to

Suburb

Park

Police station

Supermarket

Hospital

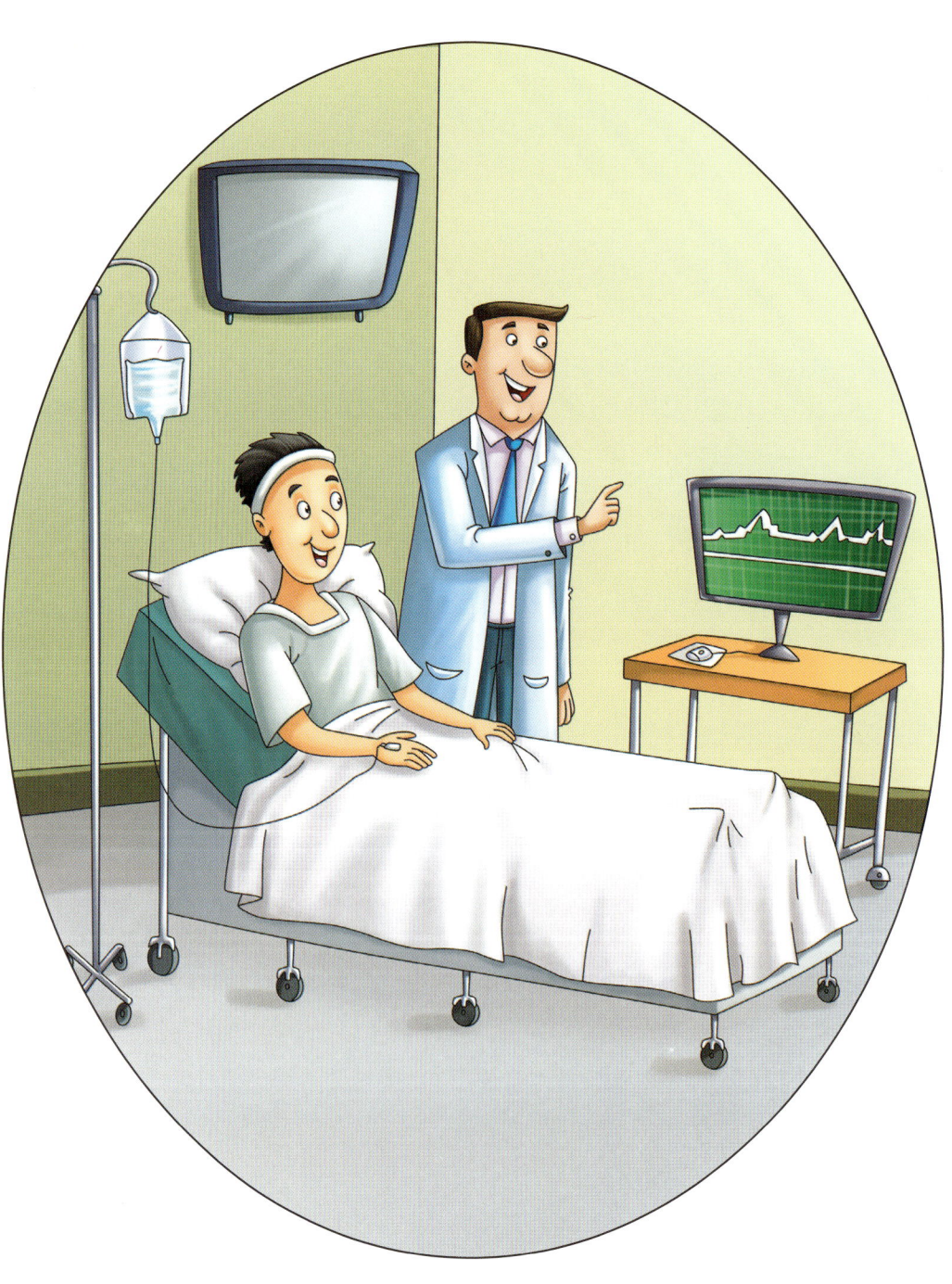

Post office

Pharmacy

School

Ice cream parlour

Bank

Bakery

Railway station

Airport

Bus station

Theatre

Amusement park

Movie hall

Zoo

Museum

Gymnasium

Petrol pump

Skyscrapers

Car park

College

Court

Book store

Public library

Flyovers

Gas station

Hotels

Restaurants